?
HOW

HISTORY OPENS WINDOWS

The AZTECS

JANE SHUTER

Heinemann Library
Chicago, Illinois

Designed by Roslyn Broder
Printed in Hong Kong

06 05 04 03 02
10 9 8 7 6 5 4 3 2 1

Library of Congress Cataloging-in-Publication Data
Shuter, Jane.
  The Aztecs / Jane Shuter.
    p. cm. – (History opens windows)
Includes bibliographical references and index.
Summary: Presents an overview of the Aztec culture, discussing their government, recreation, trade, travel, family life, food, occupations, and entertainment.
  ISBN 1-58810-589-X (lib. bdg.)   ISBN 1-4034-0024-5 (pbk. bdg.)
  1. Aztecs – History – Juvenile literature. 2. Aztecs – Social life and customs – Juvenile literature. [1. Aztecs. 2. Indians of Mexico.]
  I. Title. II. Series.
F1219.73 .S56 2002
972'.01 – dc21
                                   2001004026

Acknowledgments
The author and publishers are grateful to the following for permission to reproduce copyright material:
p. 6 Bridgeman Art Library/Biblioteca Medicea-Laurenziana, Florence; p. 8 Mireille Vautier/The Art Archive/National Archives, Mexico; p. 9 Museum fur Volkerkunde, Vienna/Werner Forman/Art Resource; p. 10 Archivo Iconografico, S.A./Corbis; p. 11 Charles and Josette Lenars/Corbis; p. 12 Pigorini Museum of Prehistory and Ethnography, Rome/Werner Forman/Art Resource; p. 14 Bridgeman Art Library/British Library, London; pp. 16, 28 Werner Forman/Art Resource; pp. 17, 29 National Museum of Anthropology, Mexico City/Werner Forman/Art Resource; p. 18 Bettmann/Corbis; p. 20 The Art Archive; p. 21 Corbis; p. 22 Ancient Art & Architecture; pp. 23, 25 The Art Archive/Biblioteca Nacional Madrid/Dagli Orti; p. 24 Scala/Art Resource; p. 26 Giraudon/Art Resource; p. 27 Michel Zabe/Art Resource; p. 30 Mireille Vautier/The Art Archive/Antochiw Collection, Mexico

Illustrations: p. 4 Eileen Mueller Neill; pp. 7, 13, 15, 19 David Westerfield
Cover photograph courtesy of The Art Archive/Biblioteca Nacional Madrid/Dagli Orti

Every effort has been made to contact copyright holders of any material reproduced in this book. Any omissions will be rectified in subsequent printings if notice is given to the publisher.

Some words are shown in bold, **like this.** You can find out what they mean by looking in the glossary.

Contents

Introduction

This map shows lands the Aztecs ruled in about 1500.

4

The Aztecs were a group of people who became powerful in Central America starting in about 1430. They had no settled home until they built the city of Tenochtitlán on Lake Texcoco, in modern Mexico, in about 1325. From then on they became more and more powerful.

At first, the Aztecs took control of the area around Tenochtitlán. They did this by making **alliances** with other groups, such as the lords of Texcoco, who were very powerful in the area. When the Aztecs were strong enough, they began to take over by force instead. By 1500 they controlled a large part of modern Mexico. By the time the Spanish arrived in 1519, the Aztec leader, Montezuma II, ruled a rich **empire** of more than a million people.

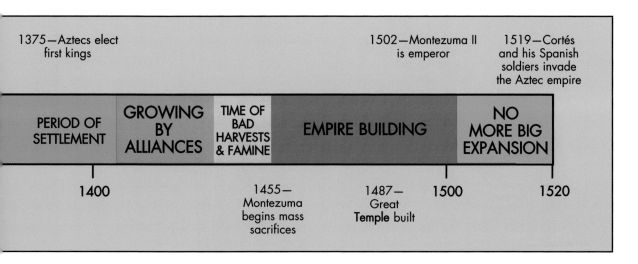

How Were the Aztecs Ruled?

Early Aztecs lived, worked, and ran their lives in groups of related families, called *calpulli.* Their ruler, the *tlatoani* ("he who speaks"), was chosen by a council of people from each *calpulli.* He made big decisions and was a war leader. But the heads of each *calpulli* ran daily life.

As the Aztec **empire** grew, the Aztecs began to organize life not in *calpulli,* but by levels of importance. The higher up the "pyramid of power" you were, the more important you were.

The Aztecs had laws about crimes, property ownership, and even marriage and divorce. This Aztec painting shows four judges deciding the punishments for the two criminals in the middle.

Emperor

Chief Adviser

Nobles

War Leaders

Governors

Merchants

Priests

Scribes

Craft Workers

Priests/
Priestesses

Farmers

Builders

Temple
Workers

Workers

Slaves

7

War

The Aztecs had to be good fighters to take over other groups and keep their **empire** together. When the Aztecs decided to take over another group, they gave those people three chances to join the Aztec empire. If they did not, the priests chose a good day to fight and the army attacked at dawn. Battles were fought hand-to-hand. The Aztecs usually won.

Starting at age fifteen, boys were trained to fight in case there was a war. There was no permanent army, but all men had to be ready to fight. **Nobles** led the army. The most important were the Eagle Knights and the Jaguar Knights.

*This is a picture list of some of the **tributes** that cities in the Aztec empire had to send to Tenochtitlán. It shows some of the things the Aztecs saw as valuable.*

This shield probably belonged to the ruler Ahuitzotl. The wooden back is decorated with a beautiful pattern of a fierce animal.

Each **calpulli** had a storehouse for weapons and armor. The head of the *calpulli* had to make sure there were enough weapons and armor and that everything was kept in good repair.

The Aztecs fought with stone-tipped spears and clubs. They also used slings and bows with stone-tipped arrows. Their armor was made of padded cotton, soaked in salt water to stiffen it. The armor was often painted or decorated with feathers. Aztec shields were made from wood and leather, or cloth. They were often decorated.

9

Religion

The Aztecs believed in many different gods and goddesses who controlled every part of life. Some were more powerful than others. All of them needed to be kept happy with prayers, music, and dancing. They also needed to be given things—food, gifts, but most of all, human blood. Without gifts of blood the gods would stop the rain, the sun, and everything else. Often priests and other people in the city would give some of their blood in a bowl. But sometimes the gods wanted a whole life. The Aztecs believed that it was an honor to be sacrificed.

This carved stone head shows the Moon goddess. The circles on her cheeks are bells, because the Aztecs also called her "Lady Golden Bells."

The Aztecs told many stories about the gods. One of these stories was about the white-skinned Feathered Serpent god, Quetzalcoatl, who had created humans. He was the only god who was against human sacrifice. He tried to stop the Aztecs from making human sacrifices. But the Aztecs thought that if they stopped, the world would end. So Quetzalcoatl sailed away, to the east. The story said that he would come back in the year Reed One, or 1519. This story would have a terrible effect when 1519 came.

This picture shows the modern remains of the Temple of the Sun, built in Teotihuacán by the Aztecs.

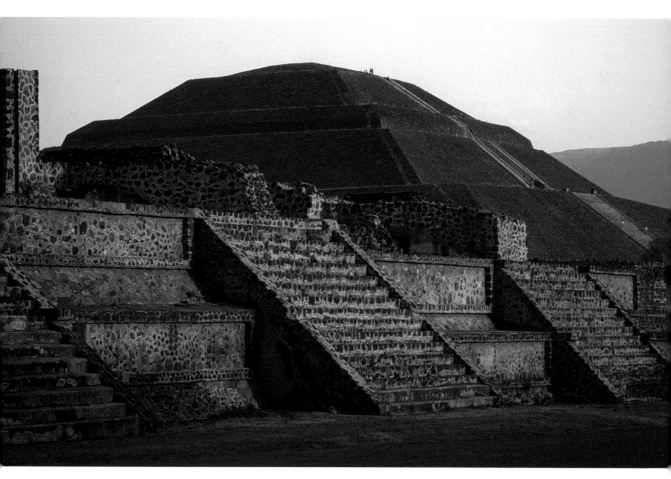

Temples and Buildings

Temples were the homes of the gods, so they were the biggest and best decorated of all Aztec buildings. They had to be tall, reaching up to the gods in the sky. They had to be at the center of a city, because the Aztecs had five directions: north, south, east, west, and center. The center was where this world joined the world of the gods and the different worlds the Aztecs believed they went to after death. So temples were built in a walled temple area in the center of the city, with gates to the north, south, east, and west.

*This is the handle of a knife that was used for sacrifices in religious **ceremonies.***

The Templo Mayor in Tenochtitlán was built for two important Aztec gods.

The **shrine** to the rain god, Tlaloc, was decorated with blue stripes.

The shrine to the war god, Huitzilopochtli, was decorated with white skulls.

The temple was in the great square in the center of the city and was surrounded by other temples.

13

Cities

Aztec cities were divided into different areas. The walled **temple** area was at the center of the city. Spreading out from this area were royal palaces, homes of important **nobles,** traders' homes, and the homes and workshops of craft workers and ordinary people. These were all in different "wards," each based on *calpulli* and run by its own officials.

The largest and most important Aztec city was Tenochtitlán. Built on Lake Texcoco, it was the first Aztec city. It grew so much that it reached Tlateloco, the other city on the lake. Both these cities had **canals** as well as roads.

This early European map of Tenochtitlán was made shortly after the Spanish invasion.

Temples, palaces, and important public buildings were made of stone.

Important buildings were carved and painted, inside and out.

There were paved roads and paved open spaces called plazas.

Temples were regularly rebuilt in the same place, over the old one, so they became higher and higher.

15

Trade and Travel

The Aztecs traveled on foot or in canoes. They did not ride animals or use wheeled carts. Even traders, who traveled a long way, walked if they could not travel by water. The Aztecs traded in two ways.

Ordinary people went to market and traded pots, food, or anything else they had grown or made for things they wanted.

Pochetecatl, or traders, had their own rules and levels of importance. They brought back raw materials, like precious stones, that craft workers needed. They also brought things that only the **emperor** or his **nobles** could buy. They also explored other lands for the emperor.

This is an Aztec drawing of a trader, from an Aztec book. Traders had to carry everything on their backs, unless they were important enough to have a servant or slave to carry things for them.

Every Aztec village, town, and city had at least one market. The market at Tlateloco was the biggest. All markets had the same rules. Instead of using money, the Aztecs **bartered.** They could also use cocoa beans or lengths of cloth to make up any difference in value.

Breaking the rules about fair prices meant punishment in the local court. In large markets, everyone selling the same thing sat together.

This modern recreation shows part of a town market.

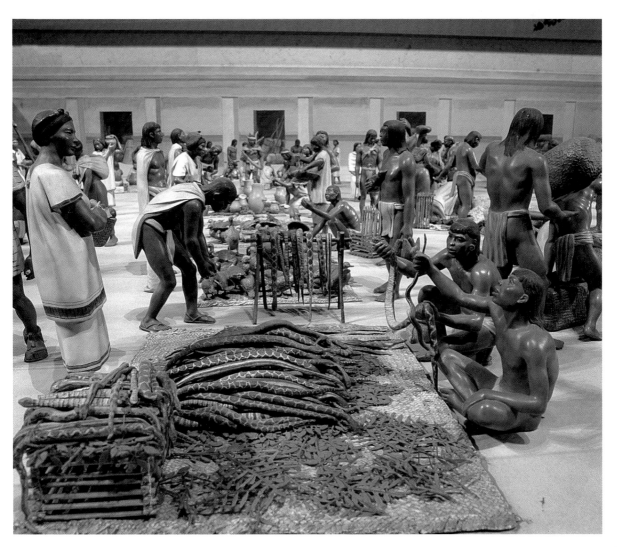

Food and Farming

Aztec farmers grew corn to make flour and *atolli,* a porridge that was often flavored with honey or chilis. They also grew chilis, peppers, beans, squash, onions, tomatoes, sweet potatoes, and cocoa beans. They kept turkeys and dogs for meat and also hunted wild animals like deer and rabbits.

Only important people ate meat every day. Ordinary people ate more fish and seafood than meat. However, ordinary people mostly ate *atolli* and flat bread, tortillas, or tamales, wrapped around vegetables. Women did the cooking over an open fire. They cooked mostly stews or mixtures cooked in a pot on the open flames. Whole fish and meat could be roasted.

This drawing shows an Aztec farmer weeding his corn plants with a digging stick.

Tenochtitlán grew by making land for houses and farming on **chinampas.** Even with *chinampa* fields, they did not grow enough to feed everyone. But they did not have to buy as much as they would have without the *chinampas.*

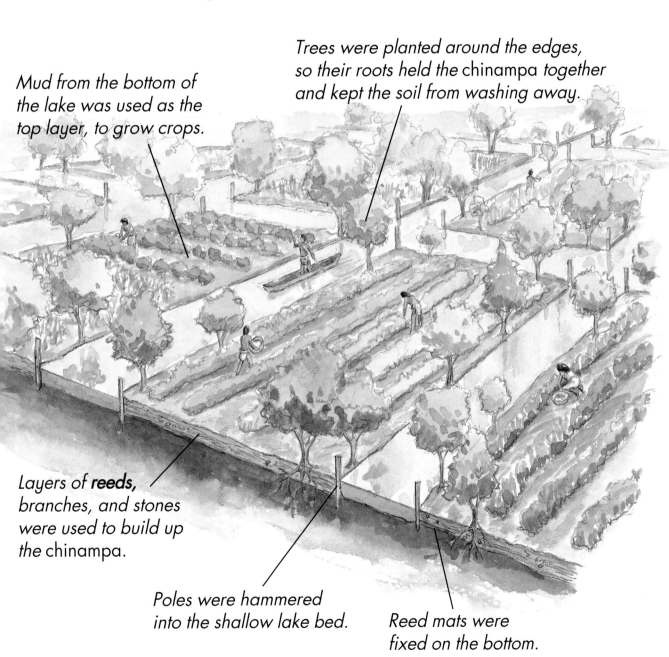

Trees were planted around the edges, so their roots held the chinampa *together* and kept the soil from washing away.

Mud from the bottom of the lake was used as the top layer, to grow crops.

Layers of **reeds,** branches, and stones were used to build up *the* chinampa.

Poles were hammered into the shallow lake bed.

Reed mats were fixed on the bottom.

19

Families

The Aztecs lived and worked in family groups called *calpulli.* In towns and villages, most people lived in simple rectangular houses built from mud bricks with a **reed** roof. They had a door, but no windows. The floor was made of cement that was painted red and polished. There was a **hearth** for cooking and a stone to grind corn. People sat on mats or straw cushions.

A young man married in his early twenties, usually to a younger girl. The wedding was an important occasion for the *calpulli.* Babies were very important to the Aztecs. A woman who died in childbirth had the same funeral as a warrior killed in battle.

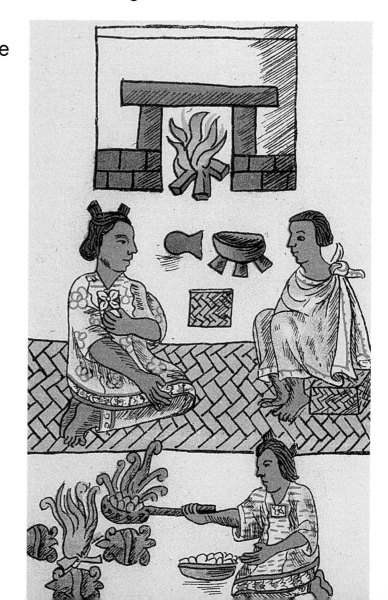

This picture shows a husband and wife in their home. The husband, as the most important person in the family, has a stool to sit on. Most people sat on the ground, on mats.

This picture shows how most children were educated. A father is teaching his son how to fish, while the mother teaches her daughter how to weave.

Aztec men worked and fought while women cared for the home and the family. Children were brought up to follow their parents. Boys learned their fathers' trades, and girls learned to run a home.

Boys from important families, as well as some clever boys from ordinary families, went to one of the special schools that trained them to be priests, **scribes,** or warriors. Most boys from ordinary families went to a local school to learn how to fight. Everyone had to learn the songs and dances for religious **festivals.** The House of Song, where these were taught to children between twelve and fifteen, was the only school that girls went to.

21

Clothes

Most of the Aztecs' clothes were made from cotton dyed with vegetable dyes. The clothes were made by folding and tying a piece of cloth. All men wore **loincloths,** and some of them also wore skirts. Women wore long skirts and **tunics.** Most people also wore a *tilmatli*—a cape tied at the shoulder.

Even though everyone wore the same style of clothes, it was easy to tell how important a person was. Priests tied their loincloths in a different way. The most important people wore the most brightly colored, patterned, and decorated clothes.

This beautiful headdress is a copy of one that was worn by Montezuma.

This painting of Montezuma and a priest was made by a Spanish artist soon after the Spanish arrived. It shows the types of clothes that important people wore.

There were laws about what people wore. You could tell what job people did by the clothes they were wearing. Capes had the most rules. Ordinary people could not wear cotton capes. They had to wear capes made from leaf fibers from various plants. There were rules about length, color, pattern, and even how it was tied.

Clothing rules also applied to shoes, hairstyles, and jewelry. For example, **nobles** wore decorated leather sandals while ordinary people wore sandals of woven leaves.

23

Entertainment

Some Aztec sports and games were only played by one group of people. Only **nobles** could play *tlachtli,* a ball game that was similar to one that the Maya played. It was played on a long thin court with stone walls along the long sides. Each team tried to get a rubber ball to the other team's end of the court. They could bounce it off people and the walls, but they could not let it touch the ground. The game could be won at any time by throwing the ball through stone rings on the side walls that were just big enough for the ball to go through. This game was mainly played at religious **festivals.**

These Aztecs are playing patolli. This was a game where people raced bean counters around a board. Everyone could play this game.

Music was very important to the Aztecs. Singing, dancing, and music were part of almost all religious festivals. All children had to learn the songs and dances for the religious festivals. They were expected to join in when the festivals were held and to know just what to sing and do.

Because music was such a big part of the Aztec religion, the Spanish destroyed most Aztec musical instruments when they tried to stamp out their religion. But there are still pictures from the time to show the kinds of instruments the Aztecs played. The most important of these were drums, rattles, and pipes.

This pictures shows Aztecs dancing at a religious festival. The drummers in the middle are playing two different kinds of drums.

Writing and Calendars

The Aztecs spoke a language called *Nahuatl*. They also had a separate written language that used pictures called glyphs. They wrote painted folding books, called codices, on bark paper. Few people could read, and even fewer could write. Some boys trained as **scribes** in special schools where they learned to draw glyphs. They had to learn many rules about color and size. Some glyphs were simple—for example, footprints meant travel. But many glyphs were meant to remind people of a story they had been told by showing a single, important scene from that story.

This is part of a codex—you can see the fold line on the right side of the big picture. The big picture is the "reminding" scene.

This stone shows part of the Aztec sacred calendar. The face in the center is the Sun god.

The Aztecs had two calendars. The "sacred calendar" had 260 days. These combined 20 names and 13 numbers in a complicated system, which repeated itself after 260 days.

The second calendar was the seasonal calendar that the Aztecs used to decide when to plant and harvest crops. It was based around the number twenty because that is how many fingers and toes a person has. It had 18 months of 20 days each, making a 360-day year. Each month had a **festival** for a particular god. The year was completed with five unlucky days, which had no name or god.

Crafts

The first Aztecs were self-supporting, meaning that they made or grew everything they needed. But as their **empire** grew and markets became an important part of daily life, more and more people specialized in making just one thing.

Specializing meant that craft workers became more skilled at their trade. This could be anything from building to making pots, to making jewelry or working with feathers. In cities, craft workers lived in a particular area with the other families, often from the same *calpulli,* who had the same skill.

*Jewelers like the one that made this ornament were important. The most skilled of them often worked just for the **emperor** in workshops in the palace.*

Craft workers who made gold and silver jewelry and offerings for the gods were probably the most important of all craft workers. They worked just for the emperor, **temples,** and **nobles.** The Mixtec people, who had been taken over by the Aztecs, were the most skillful gold workers. Mixtec **tribute** was often paid mainly in gold, although other Aztec craft workers learned Mixtec techniques. It was stories of gold that led the Spanish to try to take over the Aztec empire.

This piece of gold jewelry was made by the Mixtecs. The Sun god is in the center of the circle.

End of Empire

The year 1519 was when the Aztecs believed the god Quetzalcoatl would return with an army. When the **emperor** Montezuma heard that an army had arrived, he did not know what to do. Was their leader, Hernán Cortés, a god or an enemy? Montezuma decided to greet him as a god, just in case.

By the time he realized Cortés was an enemy, it was too late. He had welcomed Cortés and his men into Tenochtitlán. He tried to get rid of the Spanish. But they had horses, cannons, guns, and help from people the Aztecs had taken over. Also, the Aztecs still fought to capture, while the Spanish killed as many Aztecs as they could. By 1521 the Spanish had killed all the Aztecs or made them slaves.

This Aztec picture shows a Spanish attack. With the advantage of horses and guns, the Spanish were able to beat the Aztecs.

Glossary

alliance agreement between groups or countries to protect and help each other

barter to trade one thing for another without using money

calpulli group of families who lived and worked together

canal deep ditch filled with water that is used for boats or for irrigation

ceremony set of acts with religious meaning

chinampa piece of land for growing crops that is built to float on top of a lake

emperor ruler who has total power, like a king

empire group of territories or lands controlled by one country

festival time of celebration with special events and entertainment

hearth flat bed of stones for lighting a fire on

loincloth short skirt that covers the part of the body between the waist and thighs

noble important person of high birth or rank

reed tall, thick grass that grows in wet areas

scribe person whose job is to read, write, and keep records

shrine special place for worshiping gods or dead relatives

temple building that is the home of gods and goddesses, where people pray to them

tribute payment made by one ruler or group of people to another, usually to keep peace

tunic garment shaped like a knee-length T-shirt

More Books to Read

Ganeri, Anita. *The Aztecs.* Austin, Tex.: Raintree Steck-Vaughn, 2000.

Kimmel, Eric A. *Montezuma & the Fall of the Aztecs.* New York: Holiday House, Inc., 2000.

Reid, Struan. *Montezuma.* Chicago: Heinemann Library, 2002.

Pronunciation Guide

atolli   ah-TOLL-lee

calpulli   kal-POOL-lee

chinampa   chi-NAM-pah

Huitzilopochtli   weet-zeel-oh-POCH-tlee

Montezuma   mon-te-ZOO-mah

Nahuatl   nah-hoo-AH-tul

patolli   pah-TOLL-lee

pochetecatl   poh-che-te-KAH-tul

Quetzalcoatl   ket-zal-co-AH-tul

Tenochtitlán   ten-och-teet-LAN

tlachtli   tlach-tlee

Tlaloc   tlah-lock

tilmatli   teel-MAT-lee

tlatoani   tlah-to-AH-nee

Index